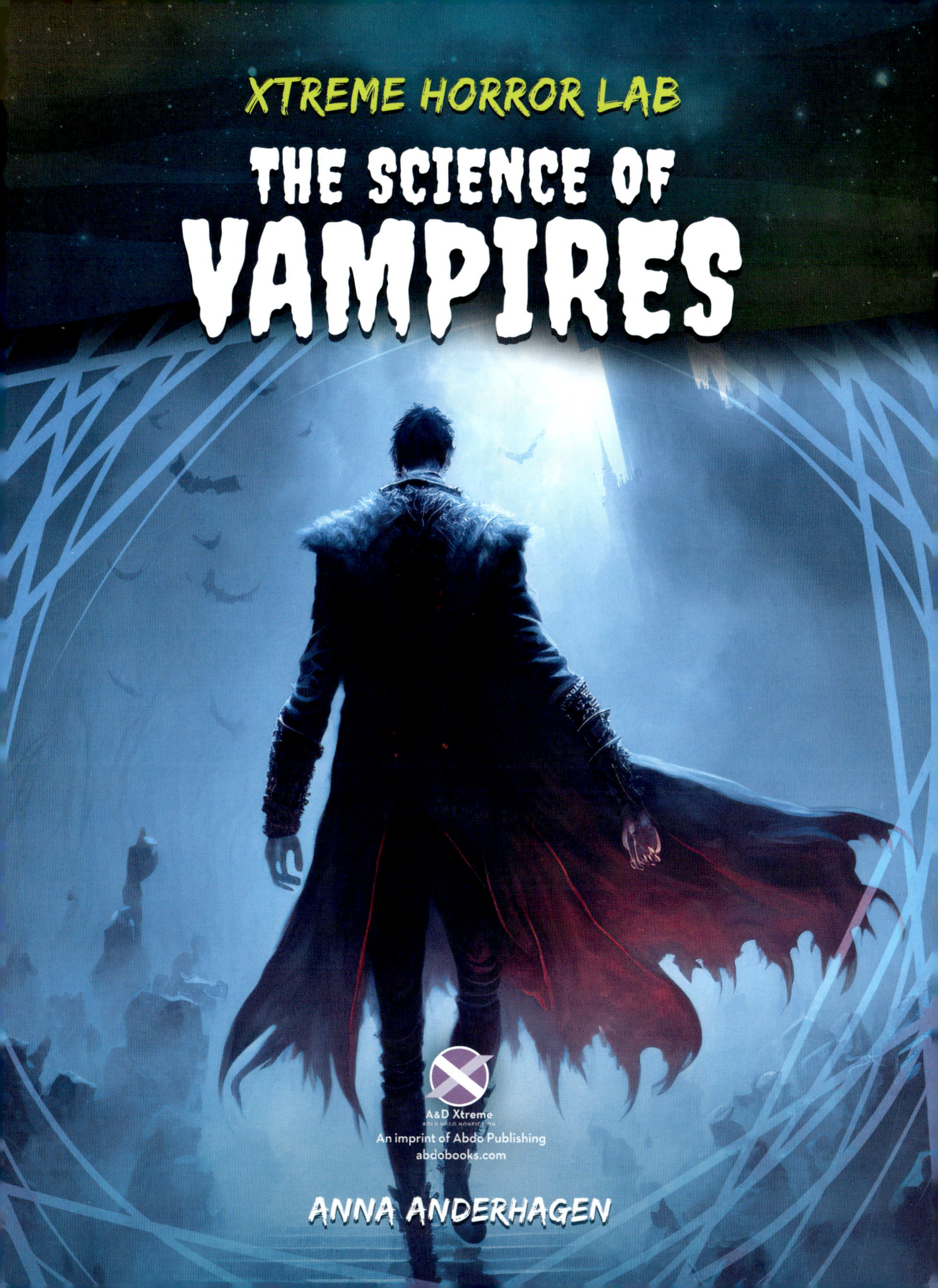

XTREME HORROR LAB

THE SCIENCE OF VAMPIRES

A&D Xtreme
An imprint of Abdo Publishing
abdobooks.com

ANNA ANDERHAGEN

TAKE IT TO THE XTREME!

GET READY FOR AN EXTREME ADVENTURE! THE PAGES OF THIS BOOK WILL TAKE YOU INTO THE SPOOKY WORLD OF UNEXPLAINED PHENOMENA. WHEN YOU HAVE FINISHED READING THIS BOOK, TAKE THE XTREME CHALLENGE ON PAGE 43 ABOUT WHAT YOU'VE LEARNED!

ABDOBOOKS.COM
Published by Abdo Publishing, a division of ABDO, PO Box 398166, Minneapolis, Minnesota 55439.

Printed in the United States of America, North Mankato, MN
052024
092024

THIS BOOK CONTAINS RECYCLED MATERIALS

Design: Kelly Doudna, Mighty Media, Inc.
Production: Mighty Media, Inc.
Editor: Jessica Rusick
Cover Photograph: Jacques Evangelista/Adobe Stock
Interior Photographs: aliaksei kruhlenia/Shutterstock Images, pp. 16-17; alswart/Adobe Stock, p. 45 (bottom); AlyoshinE/Shutterstock Images, pp. 36-37; Cbarry123/Wikimedia Commons, p. 25; David Henry Friston / Wikimedia Commons, pp. 20-21; dblumenberg/Adobe Stock, pp. 40-41; DR HAROUT TANIELIAN/Science Source, p. 39; fotogal/Adobe Stock, p. 45 (top); FOTOKITA/Shutterstock Images, pp. 4-5; Gian Bernal/ Wikimedia Commons, pp. 12-13; Gill Copeland/Shutterstock Images, pp. 28-29; Iakov Kalinin/Shutterstock Images, pp. 38-39; Jacques Evangelista/Adobe Stock, p. 1; Jakub Krechowicz/Adobe Stock, pp. 14-15; Johannes/Adobe Stock, pp. 34-35; John Phelan/Wikimedia Commons, pp. 24-25; Lebrecht Music & Arts/ Alamy Photo, pp. 8-9; Library of Congress, pp. 22-23; M Shamil/Adobe Stock, p. 44; maria_spb21/Adobe Stock, pp. 10-11; Morphart/Adobe Stock, p. 42; Natacha Pisarenko/AP Images, pp. 26-27; National Library of Medicine, p. 35; Rainer Fuhrmann/Shutterstock Images, pp. 18-19; Rights Managed/Adobe Stock, pp. 6-7, 29; SPCOLLECTION/Alamy Photo, pp. 32-33; VIAVAL TOURS/Shutterstock Images, pp. 30-31
Design Elements: Dominik Hladik/Shutterstock Images (moon); nikiteev_konstantin/Shutterstock Images (curves); pixelparticle/Shutterstock Images (stars); pixssa/Shutterstock Images (stretchy circle)

LIBRARY OF CONGRESS CONTROL NUMBER: 2023949419

PUBLISHER'S CATALOGING-IN-PUBLICATION DATA
Names: Anderhagen, Anna, author.
Title: The science of vampires / by Anna Anderhagen
Description: Minneapolis, Minnesota : Abdo Publishing, 2025 | Series: Xtreme horror lab | Includes online resources and index.
Identifiers: ISBN 9781098293239 (lib. bdg.) | ISBN 9798384912507 (ebook)
Subjects: LCSH: Vampires--Juvenile literature. | Monsters--Juvenile literature. | Vampires in popular culture--Juvenile literature. | Science--Juvenile literature.
Classification: DDC 130--dc23

TABLE OF CONTENTS

CHAPTER 1

A VAMPIRE BITE?

"Ah!" You startle awake from a scary dream. You saw a man living in a castle. He had long fangs and blood-red lips. You feel pain on the side of your neck. The spot is sore to the touch. You shiver as you remember your dream. Could you have been bitten by a vampire?

Several movies in the 1950s popularized the idea that vampires have long fangs.

CHAPTER 2

TERRIFYING TERMINOLOGY

Vampires have been said to bite victims' arms, necks, and chests.

A vampire is a **supernatural** being. Vampires are undead. This means they live after dying. Legends claim that vampires rise from their graves every night to search for fresh blood. Vampires bite their victims and suck their blood. Bitten victims turn into vampires.

Vampires are said to have many powers. They are **shape-shifters** that can change into animals such as bats. Vampires can smell blood and hear a heartbeat from miles away. They can see well in the dark too.

Vampires also have weaknesses. Sun weakens their powers. They are also said to hate garlic.

XTREME FACT

Vampire bats live in Mexico, Central America, and South America. They drink cow, pig, horse, and bird blood. They hardly ever bite people.

Actor Bela Lugosi (*right*) portrayed the vampire Count Dracula in a 1931 film. His performance inspired modern ideas about how vampires look, move, and speak.

CHAPTER 3

ANCIENT VAMPIRES

People have told stories about blood-sucking creatures for thousands of years. More than 4,000 years ago, the Babylonians believed that dead people could return as *ekimmu*. These evil beings could fly. They attacked sleeping people and sucked the life out of them.

The chupacabra is a modern vampiric legend. The creature is said to kill and suck the blood of livestock.

In ancient Greece, people told stories about a flying monster called Lamia. She was half woman and half snake. Lamia bit people and drank their blood.

Another story is from the Philippines in 900 CE. A monster called the Manananggal bit people and sucked their blood. It hated garlic.

XTREME FACT

Ancient Greek doctors used garlic to heal people from disease. Today, scientists study how garlic lowers blood pressure and helps people with blood disorders.

The Manananggal is said to have large, bat-like wings.

CHAPTER 4
EUROPEAN VAMPIRES

Vampire stories from ancient times changed over the years. During the **Middle Ages**, people told stories of undead ghosts drinking the blood of the living. Many people in Europe thought these vampiric creatures were real. These stories were passed down from generation to generation.

The word *vampire* comes from the Slavonic language. It translates to "blood monster."

Between late 1731 and early 1732, more than 20 people mysteriously died in Medveđa, Serbia. Locals blamed a vampire for the deaths. A medical officer dug up the graves of those who died. He stated that 13 people had become vampires.

Sava Savanovic is a famous Serbian vampire. He is said to live in an old mill in the village of Zarozje.

In some countries, dead bodies were buried face down to make it harder for them to escape their graves.

The villagers drove stakes through the hearts of the vampires and burned their bodies. This was a **ritual** believed to kill vampires. The story was written about in many newspapers. News of the vampires spread all over Europe.

CHAPTER 5

THE NEW ENGLAND VAMPIRE PANIC

European vampire stories reached the United States by the 1800s. The stories were often related to illness and people dying. During the 1800s, many people in Connecticut, Rhode Island, and Vermont died of tuberculosis. Some people thought it was vampires killing people, not a disease.

Vampire fiction became popular in the 1800s. One of the earliest examples is 1872's *Carmilla*, a story about a female vampire.

XTREME FACT

One of the most famous vampire stories is 1897's *Dracula*. Irish author Bram Stoker wrote the book about a powerful vampire from Transylvania, Hungary, now Romania.

Many past tuberculosis cases have been linked to vampires. It is an **infection** that attacks the lungs. People cough up blood and become very pale. Tuberculosis is spread by bacteria floating in the air.

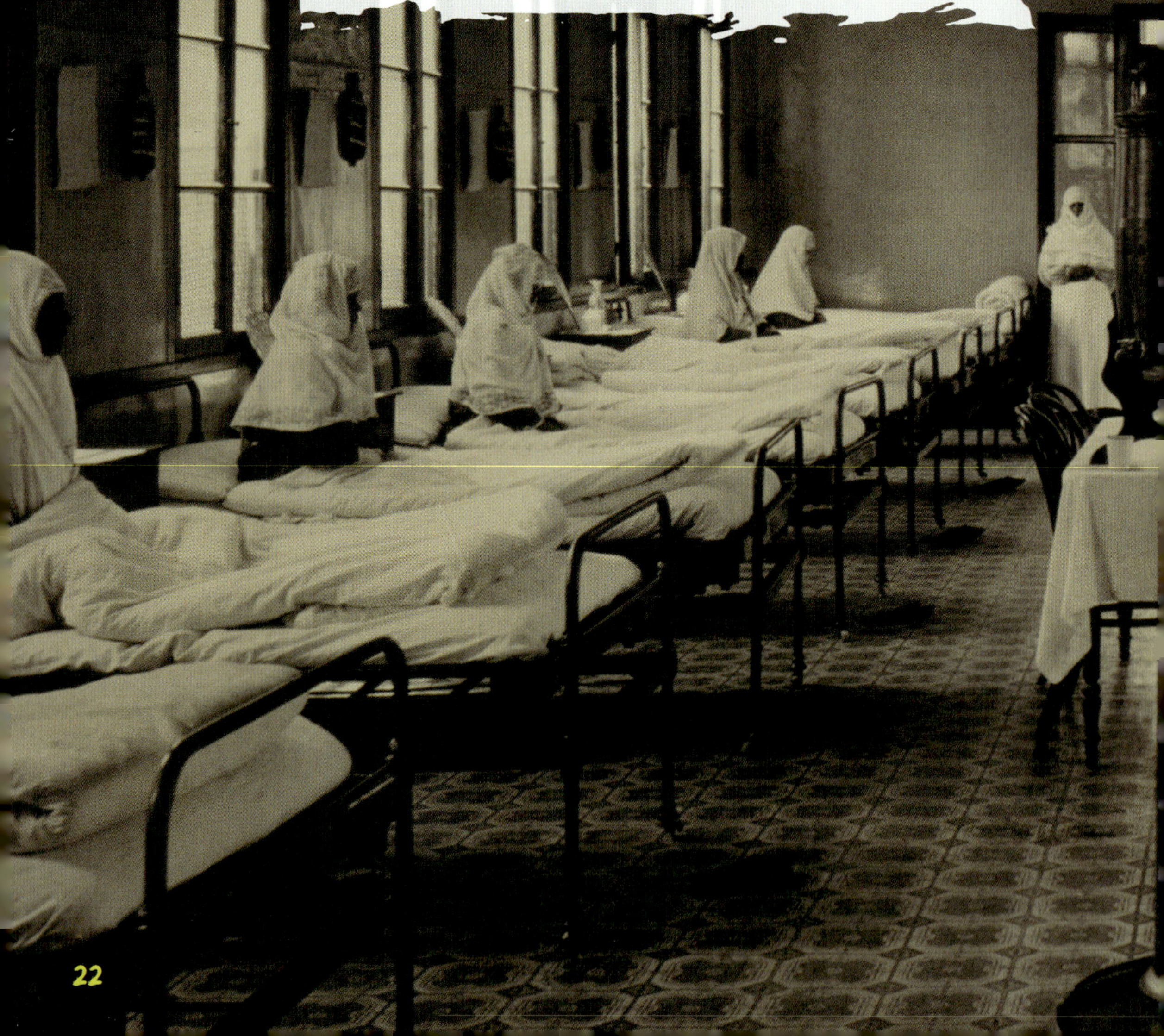

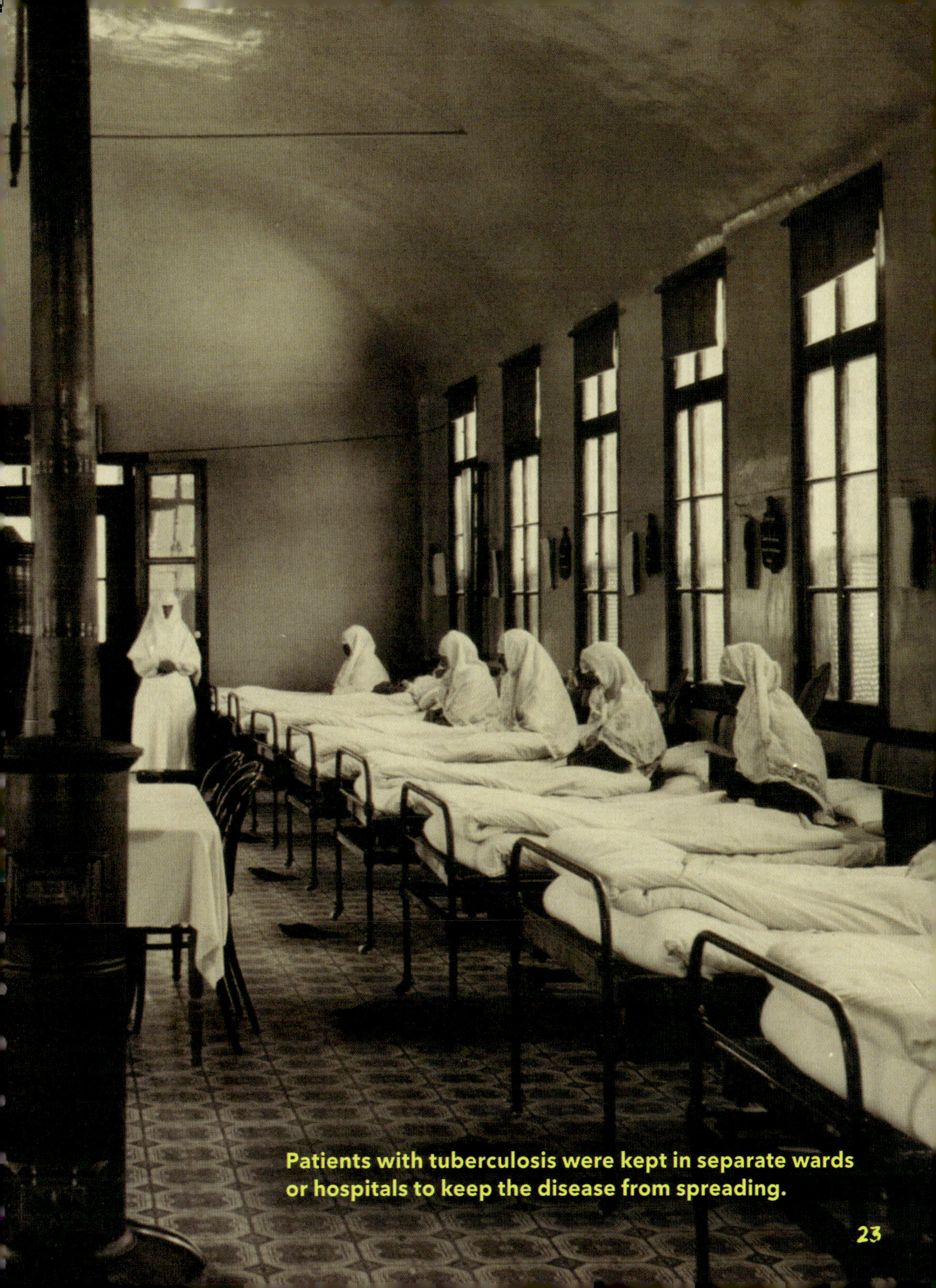

Patients with tuberculosis were kept in separate wards or hospitals to keep the disease from spreading.

The Brown family lived in Exeter, Rhode Island, in the 1880s. Mercy L. Brown, her mother, and others in the Brown family died of tuberculosis over 10 years. Many people in Exeter blamed vampires for the deaths. They believed one of the deceased Browns had become a vampire.

Members of the Brown family were buried near Chestnut Hill Baptist Church in Exeter.

Mercy L. Brown died of tuberculosis in 1892. Her mother and older sister died of the disease before her.

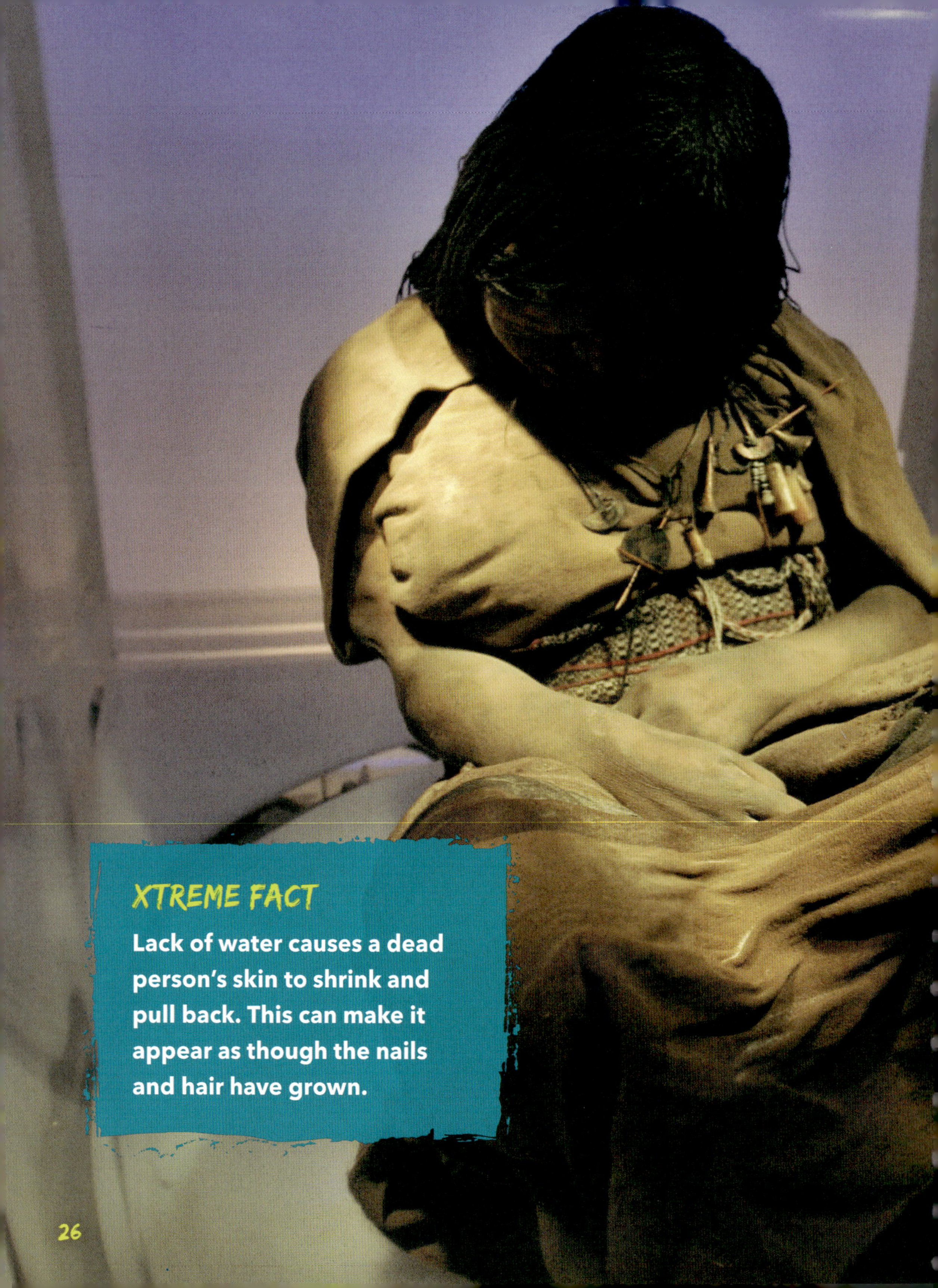

XTREME FACT

Lack of water causes a dead person's skin to shrink and pull back. This can make it appear as though the nails and hair have grown.

Some human bodies stay preserved for long periods of time. The mummy La Doncella is more than 500 years old. Dark, dry, and cold conditions kept the mummy's body in excellent condition.

The townspeople dug up the bodies of Mercy, her mother, and her sister. They found that Mercy was well-preserved. Her hair and nails appeared to have grown. She had fresh, red blood in her mouth. This made the villagers believe Mercy was a vampire. So, the villagers cut out her heart and liver and burned them. They believed this would stop her from rising.

CHAPTER 6

RITUALS & BELIEFS

Hundreds of years ago, people believed in several **rituals** to kill or stop vampires. In one ritual, after a **suspected** vampire died, people cut out the heart and liver and burned them. They might also stuff a vampire's mouth with garlic, rocks, or bricks. This was to stop a vampire from eating its way out of a grave.

One ritual to kill a vampire involved plunging a stake into the vampire's chest.

Some people thought salt or seeds could help keep vampires away. If someone thought a vampire was chasing them, they would throw salt or seeds on

the ground behind them. People believed the vampire would stop and count every fallen item. This gave the victim time to escape.

The Count on a parade float at SeaWorld in Florida. The Count is a vampire character from the children's show *Sesame Street* who loves to count. The character's name is a pun on the famous vampire Count Dracula.

CHAPTER 7

WHY DID PEOPLE BELIEVE?

Plague outbreaks in Europe were often blamed on vampires or other undead creatures.

People believed in vampires for several reasons. It was a common belief that **misfortunes** were caused by the undead. Some people even believed that a dead person could harm the living. So, many people were afraid of the dead. If something bad happened, they thought a dead person must be responsible.

Hundreds of years ago, people also did not know that germs caused illness and death. They did not understand how diseases spread. So, they blamed **supernatural** forces such as vampires instead.

In 1882, German physician Dr. Robert Koch discovered the bacteria that causes tuberculosis. However, many people continued to blame the disease on vampire attacks.

Finally, people did not understand how bodies **decompose**. For example, it is common to find blood in a dead person's mouth. That's because decomposition gases can push blood out of the intestines. This natural process can make it look like a dead person has recently sucked blood.

It usually takes 10 to 15 years for a buried body to decompose into a skeleton. The time it takes depends on how and where the body was buried.

CHAPTER 8

VAMPIRIC DISEASES

Several diseases may also have been mistaken for vampirism. Porphyria is a blood disorder. People with porphyria are very sensitive to sunlight. They may also develop bone problems over time, causing the teeth to change color.

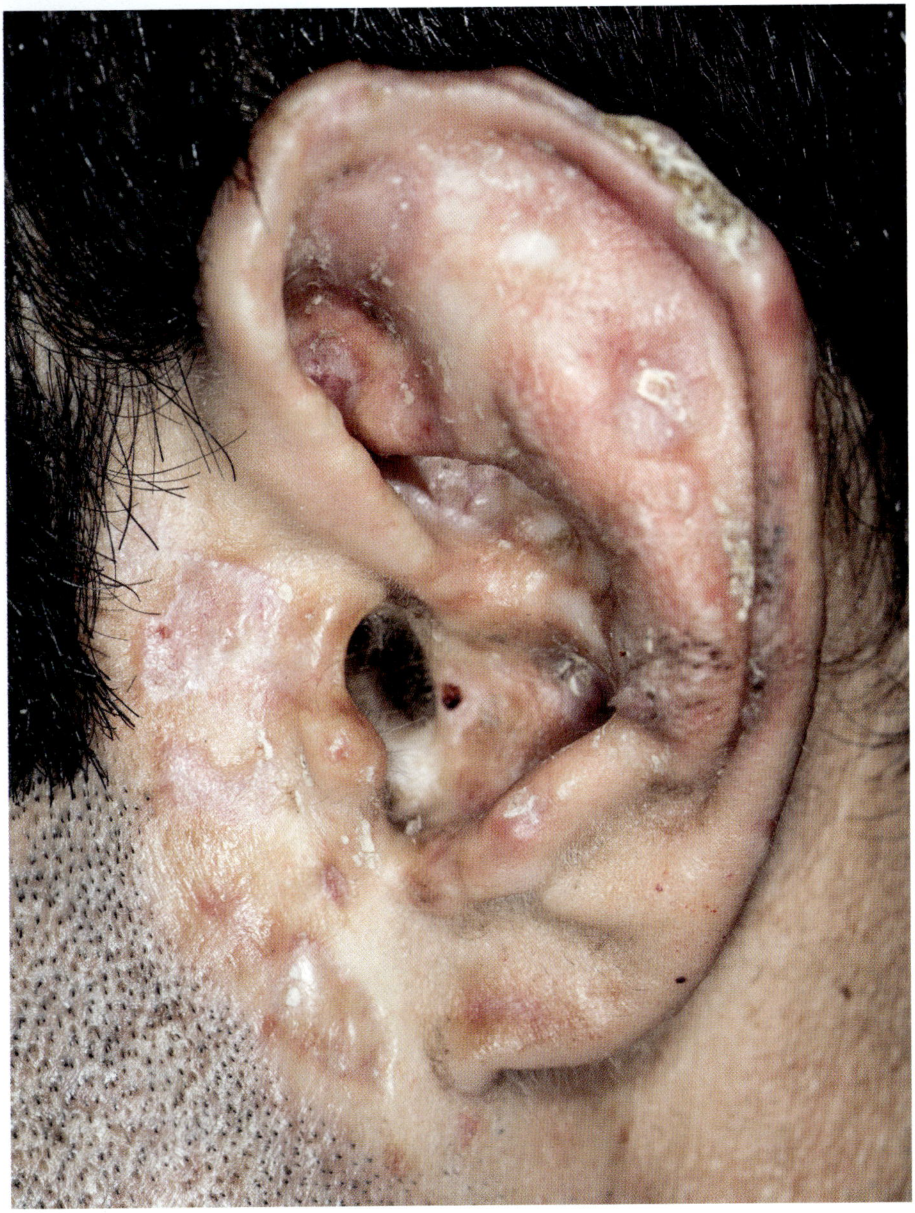

People with porphyria can develop painful rashes, burns, and blisters after sun exposure.

Rabies is another disease associated with vampires. People get rabies after being bitten by an animal **infected** with the rabies virus. Many rabies symptoms describe vampire behavior. The symptoms can include acting strangely, having bloody **saliva**, and hating **pungent** smells such as garlic.

Bats, wolves, and dogs are common rabies carriers. These animals are also associated with vampires in legends.

CHAPTER 9

SCIENCE VS. STORIES

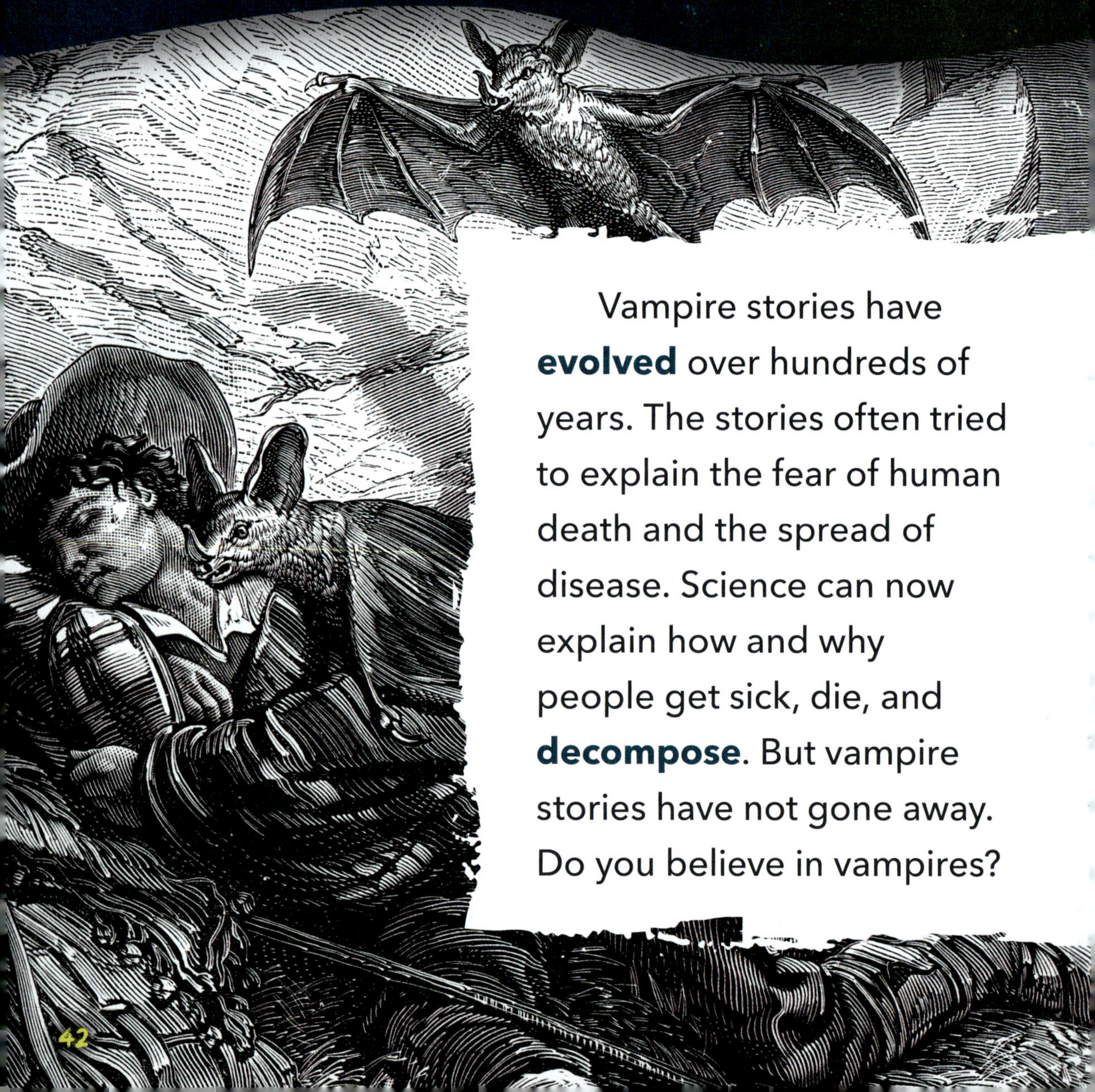

Vampire stories have **evolved** over hundreds of years. The stories often tried to explain the fear of human death and the spread of disease. Science can now explain how and why people get sick, die, and **decompose**. But vampire stories have not gone away. Do you believe in vampires?

XTREME CHALLENGE

TAKE THE QUIZ BELOW AND PUT WHAT YOU'VE LEARNED TO THE TEST!

1) What is a vampire?

2) What are traits associated with vampires?

3) Why do you think people believed in vampires?

4) What diseases are associated with vampires?

5) After reading this book, do you believe in vampires?

VAMPIRE HORROR LAB

Create **decomposition** gases using bananas and blueberries!

WHAT YOU NEED

- 2 small empty water bottles
- knife and cutting board
- fork
- 2 balloons
- water
- banana with peel
- ½ cup blueberries

WHAT YOU DO

1. Peel the banana. Have an adult help you cut the peel into small pieces. Mash the banana into small pieces with the fork.

2. Insert the mashed banana and cut peel pieces into one bottle.

3 Mash the blueberries with the fork. Insert the mashed blueberries into the other bottle.

4 Fill each bottle with water. Make sure there is no air at the top.

5 Fit an uninflated balloon over the mouth of each bottle. Place the bottles in a sunny spot.

6 Check your bottles each day for a week. What do you notice?

WHAT HAPPENED?

Organic material **decomposes** over time. When it decomposes without air, the material produces a gas called methane. This gas is what filled the balloons! A dead body releases similar gases when it decomposes in a coffin.

GLOSSARY

decompose–to break down into simpler parts.

evolve–to develop gradually.

infected–to have a disease caused by bacteria or other germs. Such a sickness is an infection.

Middle Ages–a period in European history that lasted from about 500 CE to about 1500 CE.

misfortune–a bad or unlucky event.

pungent–having a strong taste or smell.

ritual–a formal act or set of acts that is repeated.

saliva–a liquid produced in the mouth. It keeps the mouth moist and helps in chewing, swallowing, and breaking down food.

shape-shifter–a mythical figure that is able to change into different forms.

supernatural–relating to magic, spirits, or other things that cannot be explained by science or nature.

suspected–thought to be guilty of something.

ONLINE RESOURCES

Booklinks
NONFICTION NETWORK
FREE! ONLINE NONFICTION RESOURCES

To learn more about vampires, please visit **abdobooklinks.com** or scan this QR code. These links are routinely monitored and updated to provide the most current information available.

INDEX